First World War
and Army of Occupation
War Diary
France, Belgium and Germany

32 DIVISION
Headquarters, Branches and Services
Royal Army Ordnance Corps
Deputy Assistant Director Ordnance Services
1 January 1919 - 30 November 1919

WO95/2379/3

The Naval & Military Press Ltd
www.nmarchive.com
Published in association with The National Archives

Published by

The Naval & Military Press Ltd

Unit 10 Ridgewood Industrial Park,

Uckfield, East Sussex,

TN22 5QE England

Tel: +44 (0) 1825 749494

www.naval-military-press.com

www.nmarchive.com

This diary has been reprinted in facsimile from the original. Any imperfections are inevitably reproduced and the quality may fall short of modern type and cartographic standards.

© **Crown Copyright**
Images reproduced by permission of The National Archives, London, England, 2015.

Contents

Document type	Place/Title	Date From	Date To
Heading	Lancashire Division (Late 32nd Divn) D.A. Dir. Ordnance Serv. Jan-Nov 1919		
War Diary	In The Field	01/01/1919	26/02/1919
War Diary	Bonn	27/02/1919	31/05/1919
Miscellaneous	H.Qrs Lancs Divisional A	01/07/1919	01/07/1919
War Diary	Bonn	01/06/1919	30/09/1919
War Diary	Bonn Germany	02/10/1919	17/10/1919
War Diary	Bonn	18/10/1919	30/11/1919

LANCASHIRE DIVISION
(LATE 32ND DIVN)

D.A.D.O.S
Jan - Nov.

D. A. DIR. ORDNANCE SERV.
JAN - NOV 1919

LANCASHIRE DIVISION
(LATE 32ND DIVN)

D.A.D.O.S
Jan - Nov.

WAR DIARY or INTELLIGENCE SUMMARY

Army Form C. 2118

WO 95/322

Place	Date	Hour	Summary of Events and Information	Remarks and references to Appendices
Rouen	1.1.19		2 lorries at Railhead, one of Clothing, one with cart tralies.	
	2.1.19		Visited ADOS X Corps. Attended Pro Union Jacks from OOICT for display purposes by the troops. (As to each Bde 9 9th CPR) Tried to get stone now th Captain of Kitchen T from 2 Ordnance shops, but they haven't any. Visited Ordnance 15, 97th Bde HdQs & 10 A&S bno. no lorries.	
	3.1.19		Visited 6 Pt 1. 6 Their Kitchens. DDOS Army. 47 Ordnance Shops. Bno Visited ADO of railhead 6 one of lorries observed no response, bns contained 50 lorries. no lorries.	
	4.1.19			
	5.1.19		6 lorries of spares received. Visited HQ H.Q. Lorries. Drivers 9 in 1 Pdr HdQts. Div HdQ 15 & ANZ Army. no lorries arrived at Railhead 5.	
	6.1.19			
	7.1.19		One truck of SR'bus wheels etc (lorry bogies)	
	8.1.19		One truck of wheels horse shoes etc.	
	9.1.19		2 lorries R. Received a lorry load of Kit bags from Pro Reft. Counts for dispatch to Base.	
	10.1.19		No truck R. One load of returned Ordnance brought from Ronne. No truck. Attended Conference at ADOS X Corps. Got medal ribbon	
	11.1.19		from Matron to make presentation medals. Visited CRA & GC DAC. A load of clothing & Ordnance brought from Reception Camp.	

WAR DIARY or INTELLIGENCE SUMMARY

Army Form C. 2118

Place	Date	Hour	Summary of Events and Information	Remarks and references to Appendices
In the field	12.1.19		Two trucks arrived. One of horseshoes (900) and one of oil soak, grease, paint and picketing gear. Hoisted Amedin & Namm to get further supply of medal ribbon	
	13.1.19		One truck (open truck) of clothing, boots, gaiters, and stable necessaries. One lorry to 14th Bde. 2 lorries to Namm (37th Reception Camp) to bring back dirty blankets.	
	14.1.19		Three trucks at Railhead. Two of horseshoes, one of wheels. One lorry to 32nd Div Reception Camp to clear the railways.	
	15.1.19		No truck.	
	16.1.19		4 tons horseshoes & detail received.	
	17.1.19		No truck. Went to Namm to buy mess ribbon.	
	18.1.19		No truck. Sent one W.O. to Estry on Chances to see about stores dumped there. One lorry to Div Reception Camp.	
	19.1.19		One 12 st oil grease & soap received. Truck came with doors & windows open. Examined by me & found shattered. Two boxes of soap opened & most of the soap stolen. One lorry to 14th Bde.	
	20.1.19		No truck. One lorry to 14th Bde. One box CT to collect oil etc for emergency German guns. One to collect broken wire carrs. Bring built axle from Ba.00.34 Bm for a shed. Broken axle brought to me. One lorry to Delville oil etc to 97 Bde. One to Namm to collect chauffeurs (4)	

WAR DIARY or INTELLIGENCE SUMMARY

Army Form C. 2118

Place	Date	Hour	Summary of Events and Information	Remarks and references to Appendices
In Field	21/1/19		Two trucks one with driver for A&S H.Q. one with Boots & clothing, truck received open & looted. Sent one man to Div HdQrs to go with advance party to Germany. One lorry to 14 Bde, one lorry to deliver cleaning material to HQC & 97th Bde.	
	22/1/19		Two truck. Collected men old from 48 CCS. Visited 14, 96 & 97 Bde. Boots – Boots & Argyles, one lorry to 14 Bde, one to Div Reception Camp.	
	23/1/19		Two truck R. Went to Brussels.	
	24/1/19		Two truck R. Came back from Brussels.	
	25/1/19		Two truck R.	
	26/1/19		4 lorries Clothing & general stores. Sent off surplus wagons returned. Lys. go Field Amb. & 24 97, 17 Bde.	
	27/1/19		Two truck R. Visited OO H A T No 1 and collected 180 huts enemy papers for clearing German guns. Lorry sent to deliver oxygen cylinders at entraining station. Two truck down to Namur with stores eager for entraining Infsn. Visited CRA 97th Bde & Div HdQrs. All stores for clearing guns this.	
	28/1/19		Truck received but recognised an unsafe to accept. Visited Corps and Armt, as return of M Lorries prior to discharge.	

Army Form C. 2118

WAR DIARY
or
INTELLIGENCE SUMMARY

(Erase heading not required.)

Instructions regarding War Diaries and Intelligence Summaries are contained in F. S. Regs., Part II. and the Staff Manual respectively. Title Pages will be prepared in manuscript.

Place	Date	Hour	Summary of Events and Information	Remarks and references to Appendices
In Field	30/1/19		To Kirch. Visited Namêche to arrange time of departure & others. Visited Divisional Reptcon Comdt.	
	31/1/19		Loaded returned vehicles from Ambulances midnight Base.	

J. Kitchen Isaj
ADSS/SH

Army. Form C. 2118.

WAR DIARY
or
INTELLIGENCE SUMMARY
(Erase heading not required.)

WO 95/35

Instructions regarding War Diaries and Intelligence Summaries are contained in F. S. Regs., Part II. and the Staff Manual respectively. Title Pages will be prepared in manuscript.

Place	Date	Hour	Summary of Events and Information	Remarks and references to Appendices
	1/2/19		Sent 3 W.Os 18 O.R. + 4 loads of stores by rail to new area BONN.	
	3/2/19		Railhead SIEGBURG. No truck R. Remainder of staff by lorry to our area.	
	4/2/19		Still on the journey.	
	5/2/19		Lorries arrived at new area. Visited A.S.C. & R.A.F.C. No truck R. Truck R of 15,000 docks, horseshoes and details overdue. Visited 163 Bde R.F.A.	
	6/2/19		Visited 97th Bde. No truck R.	
	7/2/19		No truck R. Collected clothing from 4/4th Camp. Got leave for J.C. 97th Bde.	
	8/2/19		One truck received. Very badly broken. All payment parcels & own and Bay bills destroyed. Visited A + D 161, 96th Bde + Brave teatro. 20th D divine to G.O.C. 97th Bde.	
	9/2/19		No truck R. Gave staff a holiday.	
	10/2/19		No truck R.	

WAR DIARY
or
INTELLIGENCE SUMMARY

(Erase heading not required.)

Army Form C. 2118.

Instructions regarding War Diaries and Intelligence Summaries are contained in F. S. Regs., Part II. and the Staff Manual respectively. Title Pages will be prepared in manuscript.

Place	Date	Hour	Summary of Events and Information	Remarks and references to Appendices
N.S.O.	11/2/19		Drivers of lorries received. Proceed to Kuptkam (M.9) for disinfectors	
	12/2/19		No truck R. Visited 15H.F.I., horses 496 Bd.	
	13/2/19		No truck. Visited Officers Clothing for Cologne to see what items could be obtained.	
	14/2/19		No truck R.	
	15/2/19		No truck. Requisitions of Wire still going.	
	16/2/19		No truck R. Visited A.D.O.S. Corps & N.O. re trucks.	
	17/2/19		One truck. Horseshoes, wheels, 6 prs of boots, accessories. Visited Crew and registered 80 klgs 86cl wine for outfitting Sho.R.Cp.	
	18/2/19		No truck R. Requisitions & handtipping awkwine; also crockery for my totoPN.J.	
	19/2/19		5 trucks received. Euro containing underclothing for Brit.&.Ars, Clothing 10 Brit. South, grinding etc. Visited D1B.14-97 Bdc.ADOS.	
	20/2/19		No truck. Visited CCS. to buy a flannel rags for cleaning rifles as no flannelette available. None at CCS. Visited 25th Army Clothing Exchange & was promised about 1 town in 2 days time	

2449 Wt. W14957/M90 750,000 1/16 J.B.C. & A. Forms/C.2118/12.

WAR DIARY
or
INTELLIGENCE SUMMARY

Army Form C. 2118.

Place	Date	Hour	Summary of Events and Information	Remarks and references to Appendices
In the field	2/10/19		No truck R. Visited 107 Bde R.F.A.	
	20/9/19		No truck R. Sent 2 lorries to SOLAINE AUX (near Hamon) to collect 5 tons of German door powder. One truck of horseshoes. One truck R. rubber, oil, grease, camp and equipment.	
	23/9/19			
	24/9/19			
	25/9/19		No truck R. Sent rifles fitted with telescopic sights to 392 HT	
	26/9/19		No.1. Bus truck book mocharge & grindery. Lorry to Aulchoven to collect for fast travelling kitchens for Donots. Lorries returned from SOLAINE AUX with German soap powder, tole truck. Visited 13 Liverpools & One truck R, 229 Came horseshoes, toolcart. 12 L.N. Ferner (2 new Bns)	
Bonn	27/9/19			
	29/9/19			

Jno Buchan Capt

Davros 3 DAC

2449 Wt. W14957/M90 750,000 1/16 J.B.C. & A. Forms/C.2118/12.

WAR DIARY
or
INTELLIGENCE SUMMARY

Army Form C. 2118.

Place	Date	Hour	Summary of Events and Information	Remarks and references to Appendices
Bonn	1/3/19		Raiders still SIEGBURG. No truck R. Sent lorry to O.O 2nd A.T. not to draw Army Coats onto clothing. (Army Coats not available)	
	2/3/19		No truck R. Picketting gear & Soft soap & Flannelette.	
	3/3/19		No truck R.	
	4/3/19		No truck R.	
	5/3/19		Three trucks received. Clothing S.D. State necessaries. Two Shirts	
	6/3/19		No truck. Visited 4 Bde Hd Qts. Collected 11 Sets harness from various New Zeal and Divisions.	
	7/3/19		No truck. Jeans on loan to 58 Bn Manchester Regt (Young Soldiers Bn that arrived from home today) & 5 Kettles Camp & 2 Stores dryer as they without any Scouring apparatus.	
	8/3/19		One truck R. Clothing Sundry 9 nose bags. Sent 2 lorries to Saros See Zealand Division to collect vehicles.	
	9/3/19		No truck R.	
	10/3/19		No truck R.	

WAR DIARY or INTELLIGENCE SUMMARY

Army Form C. 2118.

Place	Date	Hour	Summary of Events and Information	Remarks and references to Appendices
BONN	11/3/19		To truck. Went to Cologne and requisitioned 47½ Kilos steel wire for stiffening caps. Sent lorry to pass New Zealand Div. to collect 100 kettles camp.	
	12/3/19		One tree K of horseshoes Bromo-Bass and stable necessaries. Visited J. Bn Manchesters and 6 Lancs Fusiliers.	
	13/3/19		No truck. Visited A Coy & B Coy.	
	14/3/19		No truck.	
	15/3/19		Two trucks. Tu of clothing, grindery & boots & stable necessaries, other Blacksmiths codes etc.	
	16/3/19		No truck.	
	17/3/19		No truck R. Visited 104th, Dorsets and Manchesters lecturing to them the meaning of leaving the Div. without Equipment.	
	18/3/19		Two trucks, tu of horseshoes, one truck of soap oil grease & Bromo Bass etc. Visited Bass NZ Div in exchange of rations	

Army Form C. 2118.

WAR DIARY
or
INTELLIGENCE SUMMARY
(Erase heading not required.)

Instructions regarding War Diaries and Intelligence Summaries are contained in F. S. Regs., Part II. and the Staff Manual respectively. Title Pages will be prepared in manuscript.

Place	Date	Hour	Summary of Events and Information	Remarks and references to Appendices
Or NN	19/3/19		No truck R. Visited 52 Bn Manchesters who have just arrived and are replacing Roy/L. Visited 57 Bn Manchesters	
	20/3/19		No truck R.	
	21/3/19		No truck. One truck R of Salvage despatched.	
	22/3/19		No truck. Ordered to Requisition 30 lanterns T.F. for parties conducting horses to base. Received 15 to O/c MG Horse tram party at Coln. Rmch inspected by A.A.G.H.	
	23/3/19		One truck R. Clothing, bags more & mercenaries. Indents, equipment 57th Rifle pools received from 12 Royal Scots. Equipment in very bad condition. Reported to DuMHq from any.	232.01/3/19
	24/3/19		No truck R.	
	25/3/19		No truck R. Collected various stores for travelling kitchens from DADOS NZ Div & delivered to 57th Rifle pools.	
	26/3/19		One truck R. Soap, oil, grease, camp equipment & equipment.	
	27/3/19		No truck R.	
	28/3/19		No truck R. One truck of "U" items to Base.	

WAR DIARY
INTELLIGENCE SUMMARY

Army Form C. 2118.

Place	Date	Hour	Summary of Events and Information	Remarks and references to Appendices
BONN	29/3/19		No firs R. Sent lorry to Davos N.Z. Div to collect motor travelling kitchen for awards 52nd Liverpools.	
"	30/3/19		One firs R. Relathing & table necessaries. Visited Davos 57th Liverpools.	
"	31/3/19		No firs R. Visited 96th Inf Bde.	

M. Murchand
Davos
Lancs Div

WAR DIARY or INTELLIGENCE SUMMARY

Army Form C. 2118.

DADOS

Place	Date	Hour	Summary of Events and Information	Remarks and references to Appendices
BAILN	1/4/19		One truck of dubbin, oil, grease and metalling gear.	
	2/4/19		Requisitioned 60 lanterns for use with horses going to Base.	
	3/4/19		Lieut J.J. Brade reported for duty. Major D. Parkes went on leave.	
	4/4/19		No truck. Permanent Vanish (?) in General Car. No driver.	
	5/4/19		No truck. Visited New Brutinel Depot Colgne. Visited ADOS & Corps Workshops.	
	6/4/19		No truck. Graham Attwell turned in B 53 Leyland Workshop.	
	7/4/19		Visits Franche No Stake. Staff Officers Bombing in One Truck.	
	8/4/19		Kenfroles S Park's.	
	9/4/19		No truck. Ambulances reported to ADSVS.	
	10/4/19		3 Trucks. Stores from Bn. Stn. OC. SSE	
	11/4/19		Inspected S building for New Dump	
	12/4/19		Cleared stores onwire. Main dump is to Muron	
	13/4/19		Visited 8th Infantry Brigade. New travelling kitchen on O.S. MGC Workshop issue.	
	14/4/19		No Truck. Turned in not Demob tables, 9 am R, 2" Keys, 5 a Das	
	15/4/19		One Truck of clothing	
	16/4/19		No truck. One truck of Bombing ammunition 2/6	
	17/4/19		One Truck clothing Maroun	
	18/4/19		Visited 94 Bugade	
	19/4/19		No Truck. Major Parkes returned from leave	
	20/4/19		No Truck.	

Army Form C. 2118.

WAR DIARY
or
INTELLIGENCE SUMMARY

(Erase heading not required.)

Instructions regarding War Diaries and Intelligence Summaries are contained in F. S. Regs., Part II. and the Staff Manual respectively. Title Pages will be prepared in manuscript.

Place	Date	Hour	Summary of Events and Information	Remarks and references to Appendices
BONN	21/4/19		Visited 1st Bn/Btt 6th, 5nd, 2nd Liverpools, 5th & 3rd Lancashires, Notts R.	
	22/4/19		No truck.	
	23/4/19		One truck. Visited Cologne (office of DOS) (by pw on bicycles)	
	24/4/19		No truck. Sent load of retd ordnance to Base	
	25/4/19		No truck. One truck load of repairable stores to Köln.	
	26/4/19		No truck.	
	27/4/19		One truck. Detail stores. Ambulance returned from Aust. H.Q.	
	28/4/19		No truck.	
	29/4/19		One truck. Gun cleaning, boots, clothing, stable necessaries.	
	30/4/19		No truck	

Nicholas Gray
D.A.D.O.S. Lancashire

WAR DIARY
or
INTELLIGENCE SUMMARY
(Erase heading not required.)

Army Form C. 2118.

DADOS

Place	Date	Hour	Summary of Events and Information	Remarks and references to Appendices
BONN	1/5/19		Two truck R. One truck of "U" Runners, saddlery, cargo boots etc to Calais.	
"	2/5/19		Two truck R.	
"	3/5/19		One truck R. Clothing, boots, grindery and nose bags. Visited Horse Collecting Depots & collected reports for horses to be sent to Base. One lorry to NZ Base to collect 18 sets pack saddlery.	
"	4/5/19		Two truck R.	
"	5/5/19		Two truck R. Visited 15th & 16th Lancers, Bedfords and Ottawa MGBn. re Officers + OR for attachment to Ordnance.	
"	6/5/19		One truck R. Horseshoes, oil, grease, equipment. Visited COD 16B re surplus sections. 1st Bde strength, 4,1,3 + 51. Run GP at Army Prints.	
"	7/5/19		Two truck R. Visited 51st, 52nd, 53rd Manchesters & HQ of 3rd Bde.	
"	8/5/19		Two truck. Two lorries to Railhead for Calais. Visited 42 M.V.S. 2 Cry Train + 90th Field Ambulance.	
"	9/5/19		Two lorries R. Visited 14, 95, 96, 97 Bde HQ re redistribution of Cn. to keep Kneller 1 Coy of Cn. train. Lorry to NZ Dn to collect Runners & Bicycle.	

WAR DIARY
or
INTELLIGENCE SUMMARY

Army Form C. 2118.

Place	Date	Hour	Summary of Events and Information	Remarks and references to Appendices
Bonn	10/5/19		Two trucks, bus of necessaries and clothing and boots. Visit of 192nd L.T.M Bde, 306 Field Coy, 8 Coy of 2nd ... 91st Field Amb.	
"	11/5/19		Two field kitchens arrived, one for 13 Kings, one for 5/6th Manchesters.	
"	12/5/19		One lorry to Cologne with repo. lanterns etc for Criminal enquiry party and to collect ammunition on the return journey. No truck.	
	13/5/19		No truck.	
	14/5/19		One truck. Soap, oil & grease. Visited C.O.O. re collection of Carrier Emergency Spls. was sent the wrong place, when I found the right place stores were closed.	17.15 hrs
	15/5/19		Two loads of "U" stores to Calais. Asked for cars as I have received orders to take over ceded stores. No car available. Lorry taken to collect Carrier Ammunition Emergency Spls. he tried to go to depot I visited yesterday which was wrong. Lorry journey was nil.	
	16/5/19		Two truck. Clothing, boots, grocery, necessaries & clothes equipment. Visited Ordnance Depot, A.B.A.P. Coo. & Boo. re emergency carriers & was eventually informed that none were available. Got bus to wire Calais to despatch to me.	
	17/5/19		2 loads of "R" clothing & branches to Rathlures for despatch to Koln	
	18.5.19 19.5.19		No truck. No truck.	

WAR DIARY or INTELLIGENCE SUMMARY

Army Form C. 2118

Place	Date	Hour	Summary of Events and Information	Remarks and references to Appendices
BONN	19/5/19		One lorry to Köln to collect summer underclothing. Delivered to Batts.	
"	20/5/19		One truck, horseshoes, soap, oil, grease, equipment & camp equipment.	
"	21/5/19		One lorry to Mulheim to collect K.T. body, K.T. limber & boilers without tyres. Lorry recd just before lorry departed to say not available. Lorry to Coln to collect barrack furniture clothing (drawers) delivered to Batts. Visited H. Coy train R.A.S.C. 97th Bde H.Q.rs.	
"	22/5/19		Two lorry loads of "U" stores to railhead for Calais. One lorry to Geislingen and Birlinghoven to collect ceded stocks and bring them to Bonn. Found Kraftstore at Birlinghoven had been handed over to O.T.T. Collected 5 Hargo lorries from W.O.Y.C.T.	
"	23/5/19		One lorry to Mulheim to collect 9 bicycles. Attended conference at A.D.S.	
"	24/5/19		One truck clo & gum denny. Visited 90 Field Amb. 1 Coy train R.A.S.C. 3rd T.M.B.	
"	25/5/19		No truck R.	
"	26/5/19		No truck R. One representative to take over 6 hundred GS wagons from 5 M.G.Bn at Godesberg. Equipment of 90 Field Amb. inspected. Board on ceded stocks held in annexe.	
"	27/5/19		Two trucks soap, oil, grease, horseshoes, sundries. Placed requisition orders for meat on X stencils for Nos. & 9 r.s	

Army Form C. 2118

WAR DIARY
or
INTELLIGENCE SUMMARY
(Erase heading not required.)

Instructions regarding War Diaries and Intelligence Summaries are contained in F.S. Regs., Part II. and the Staff Manual respectively. Title Pages will be prepared in manuscript.

Place	Date	Hour	Summary of Events and Information	Remarks and references to Appendices
Boden	28/5/15		No truck. Collect items for horse party from store collecting depot. One lorry to O.O x C.T. to collect Rifles.	
"	29/5/15		Three loads of returned tramware to Railhead for despatch to Calais. Fritz's 52 & 53 Manchesters	
"	30/5/15		No truck. Stores for horse conducting party sent to Kiln. Inspect ¼ closed in accordance with instructions. One lorry to collect tents from O.O.S.C.T.	
"	31/5/15		Four trucks. 2 containing fencing apparatus, one clothing, Boots, Spidery, separators, necessaries. One I.R.T. Body & Limber for 15. L.O. Visited Godesberg in exchange of I.R.T. Limber. Visited 51 Manchesters	

Inscribed Hay
Darro Lancaster

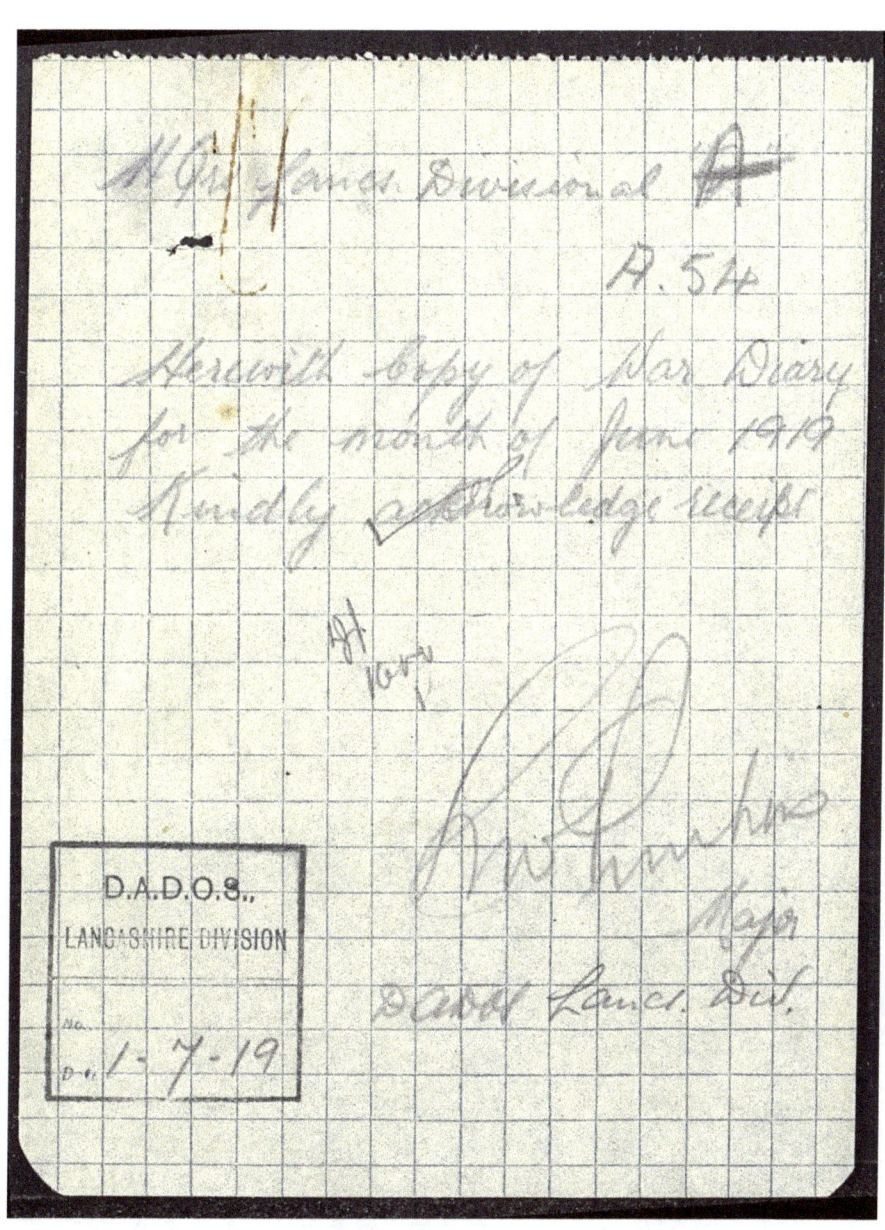

HQ Lancs Divisional

A.54

Herewith copy of War Diary for the month of June 1919. Kindly acknowledge receipt

R W Rumkin
Major
DADOS Lancs. Div.

D.A.D.O.S.,
LANCASHIRE DIVISION
1-7-19

WAR DIARY
or
INTELLIGENCE SUMMARY

(Erase heading not required.)

Army Form C. 2118

Place	Date	Hour	Summary of Events and Information	Remarks and references to Appendices
BONN	1.6.19		Visited Siegburg with platform weighing machine. Railhead supply office considered it not large enough. No church.	
"	2.6.19		Two lorries to Western Division to bring wagons. Three trucks. Two containing wheels, one of horseshoes, oil, soap & grease. Visited 5 M.G. Bn at Godesberg. Chose K.T. bodys for 53 Manchesters. q.g.s of wagon gone when sent for 12 R.N Lancs. Received sample carrier for L.T.M bombs. Said by G.O.C. it was useless & instructed to experiment however.	
"	3.6.19	11.00	Sent 9 lorries to collect vintage from Coro. Cologne. Lorries arrived at Bonn depot closed. Received new sample of Ammn Carrier for L.T.M Bombs.	
"	4.6.19		Lorries (3) to Cologne to collect tents & pillows. Visited Cologne & collected for 6" T.M collected from Bonn Railhead. Two mobile trucks. Canvas for making carriers for 9torestT.M Batteries.	
"	5.6.19		Three lorry loads of Returned stores to Railhead for Calais. Visited O.C T.M Dir List "C" Defane park Batt. 1st Bde Hd4,16,51st Kings a 206 Field Coy.	
"	6.6.19		No truck. Two loads of returned stores to Railhead for despatch to Base. Visited 51 & 53 Manchesters. A No 9, 1 Coy train RASC.	

WAR DIARY
or
INTELLIGENCE SUMMARY

(Erase heading not required.)

Army Form C. 2118

Place	Date	Hour	Summary of Events and Information	Remarks and references to Appendices
BONN	7.6.19		Attended Office of A.D.O.S. Conference Re attached R.G.A. new lorry to C.O. & C.T. followed some harness. Visited 3rd T.M.B.	
"	8.6.19		One truck containing Clothing, Boots, Gunnery, Necessaries and Towbags.	
"	9.6.19		2 Trucks of west equipment to replace leather. Visits Godesberg & allocated one truck car & 3 compleat G.S. limbers bags on Conference at D.O.S. Office on establishments replacements.	
"	10.6.19		Two trucks, one of steel (B4), bag of soap, oil, grease, horseshoes equipment & Camp equipment. Dealt over with Carl Becker & allen carriers to Sample as approved by G.O.C. for L.T.M. Brees. No truck. One lorry to X & C trs to collect 3 L.Batch shelter & delivier to 168 Bde R.F.A. 5 lorries to Cologne to collect 1 platform weighing machine for R.S.O. two Kitchens trench for 53 Manchesters and 9 Joe tents C.S.C. & 9 store tents. and 5,400 drawers cotton long, Delivered direct to battn. (Kitchens were not available.	
"	12.6.19		Three lorry loads of "N" stores to Railhead at Calais. 12 C.S.L. to T.M.C. Bns	
"	13.6.19		52 G.S.L. & 45 Shine tents to 2"A Bde, 4 Store tents to 52nd Hants to 2 C.S.L. to 219 Field by. 1 lorry to Koln to collect 2 travelly Kitchens.	

WAR DIARY
or
INTELLIGENCE SUMMARY

Army Form C. 2118

Place	Date	Hour	Summary of Events and Information	Remarks and references to Appendices
BONN	14.6.19		One truck of Clothing, Boots, Grindery, ~~Haversacks~~ Equipment, stable necessaries (1,700 towels delivered to Baths)	
"	15.6.19		No truck.	
"	16.6.19		28 tents C.S.L. 3 marquees delivered to 2nd Echelon Camp. One lorry to Cairo for horses.	
"	17.6.19		One truck, soap, oil, grease, horseshoes & equipment. One lorry to Koln to collect spare parts for M.G.mo. One to I.O.S. to collect spare parts for Inv. Guns as telegram was rec'd this morning saying 7 day for "A".	
"	18.6.19		Visited COO Koln to collect gloves anti gas. Also to find out why Guns Vickers & first aid cases were not issued; reason not available. Informed corps, & asked where to get them. No answer yet rec'd.	
"	19.6.19		Three loads of returned stores to railhead for Calais. Crew'd 1 oktr tent from 2nd Bde. Visited COO Cologne & collected 5,000 bags ration & some signalling equip authorised by GRO 3779 for 15 Lanc. F. Sound & Lanc.	
"	20.6.19		Clothing, Boots & Grindery & south drawn from Köln	

WAR DIARY
or
INTELLIGENCE SUMMARY

(Erase heading not required.)

Army Form C. 2118

Place	Date	Hour	Summary of Events and Information	Remarks and references to Appendices
BONN	21.6.19.		No truck asked for Car - none available. Drew tents (2 Marquees 18hrs) one truck of clothing, boots & groceries from Cologne. Waited eqt D/168/.	
"	22.6.19			
"	23.6.19		Visited C.O.O. Returned 2 Helios stands on loan. 2 trucks. One of stable necessaries, 9 necessaries, one Motor Car. Fr. 53 Marghetti.	
"	24.6.19		No truck.	
"	25.6.19		No truck.	
"	26.6.19		No truck. Three lorry loads of returned ordnance to Railhead. Two lorries to Köln to collect 2 lorries travelling kitchens and 1 limber for 15th & 16 Lancs. Visited C/168 & 2nd Batt HQrs.	
"	27.6.19		No truck.	
"	28.6.19		No truck. Peace signed 16 hours.	
"	29.6.19		No truck. Lieut. M. Rathmill reported for attachment to RASC.	
"	30.6.19		No truck.	
"	31.6.19.		No truck.	

R. Rutherford
Major
16/5 Lancs Fus

WAR DIARY
or
INTELLIGENCE SUMMARY
(Erase heading not required.)

Army Form C. 2118

Place	Date	Hour	Summary of Events and Information	Remarks and references to Appendices
BONN	1.7.19		One truck of medicines & horseshoes.	
"	2.7.19		No time R. Visited A.o.D. 164, C.168, 51 and 53 Manchesters.	
"	3.7.19		Holiday in celebration of peace. In spite of this 15 & 16 Lancs came in with their Jerkins & haversacks. 15 Lancs came in for tents.	
"	4.7.19.		Three lorries to Cologne to collect clothing from depot, also grinding paint shop.	
"	5.7.19		Two lorries to Cologne to collect 60 tents C.S.L. Fleas &c etc collected at 145 Bayen Strasse. Lorries then instructed to go to Wipper for the second tents. By the time lorries got there the Depot was closed and will not open again till Monday morning. 7th inst. Visited A.D.S. 2nd Bde H.Q/6. No time R.	
"	6.7.19		Visited 2 & 4 Cys Train, 52 Manchesters & 2nd Bde H.Q/6.	
"	7.7.19		6 C.S.L. tents collected from Köln. Visited 1st & 2nd Bde and Q/6.	
"	8.7.19		Two trucks. Visited D.A.P.M. 3rd Bde & Mobile Shops, 12 L.I. Lancs & Coy Train. Returned 250 respirators & 250 containers to Köln.	
"	9.7.19		One truck eqipment & Saddlery. Visited Ihrew & collected sample fuel tin for D.W.&.Q/6.	
"	10.7.19		3 loads of returned stores to railhead for despatch to Base. Visited M. & Bn, 1 Coy Train & I.C.S. 6 lorries to Eutkirchen to bring back carriages 15 pdr fitted with air recuperators for issue to batteries in lieu of	

WAR DIARY
or
INTELLIGENCE SUMMARY.

Army Form C. 2118.

Place	Date	Hour	Summary of Events and Information	Remarks and references to Appendices
BONN	11.7.19		Two loads of Jenkins to JCS. Knitted Coo Kitchen to clean & put to Bed Ti. Three loads of old horseshoes to Railhead. Nine lorries to Truck Kitchen to collect our ordinary camouflage.	
"	12.7.19		Visited ordnance stores & firms for Brigade camp. Found they were available. Went to apply to get authority.	
"	13.7.19		No truck. Visited M.G. Bn & 31st Base Schools, 57 Manchester.	
"	14.7.19		No truck. One lorry to Koln for Tarpaulins. Took indent to Div on 15th. Authority given.	
"	15.7.19		50 tailors sent to sew 9 we perform tents at a mon 15. Authority given. One truck of Harness saddlery & accessories. One lorry to collect tables form. One lorry to collect trestles from Bonn. 18 to collect the tables form. Equipment from Upper (Kola).	
"	16.7.19		Visited ADOS, OO X CT & ICS.	
"	17.7.19		1 lorry to Koln to collect 5 "Geo". Railhead with "U" stores	
"	18.7.19		Visited DDMS Corps re tents for O.parts (n.boy) 12 L.M. lanes, 70 Field Amb (cadre) 53 Manchester, 3rd Bose Hosp 16, 57 Manchester.	
"	19.7.19		Knitted Coo Kyln re tent Bottoms. 1 lorry "V" stores to Railhead. Domis together 93 lorries clothing from Kiln.	
"	20.7.19		Holiday. Went to Koln to find laundry for blanket cleaning.	

Army Form C. 2118.

WAR DIARY
or
INTELLIGENCE SUMMARY.
(Erase heading not required.)

Instructions regarding War Diaries and Intelligence Summaries are contained in F.S. Regs. Part II. and the Staff Manual respectively. Title pages will be prepared in manuscript.

Place	Date	Hour	Summary of Events and Information	Remarks and references to Appendices
BONN	21.7.19		Visited 90 F.A. on return of bicos to England. Went to Kochen to see the first 200 blankets changed; Witness is of filling point to see exchange with units. (Three lorries employed in exchange of blankets) One lorry to collect 8 marquees delivered to Venusberg Camp. One lorry to collect 76 tent bottoms. Delivered 52 mankelos, 2 Bar Haffe, DAC, 9, 9, 2.A.	
"	22.7.19		Visited 8 A & 9.8 (borrowing tents for Bns sports) 2 lorries on blanket exchange. Three lorries on blanket exchange.	
"	23.7.19		Collected 10 marquees + 3 C.St. from 31 c.c.s for Bns sports 2 infantry units & 9 stove tent from St Markurs for Bns sports 3 lorries on blankets.	
"	24.7.19		No truck. Three lorries employed on blankets (to & from Köln) 15 lorries very late in coming in for exchange. Visited M.G. Bn. 2 lorries returning stoves to Siegberg.	
"	25.7.19		Visited 5 Borders 52 Manchesters. Three lorries on blankets.	
"	26.7.19		H.J. arrives to Köln to draw equipment. Visited Cookers + 800 offices. Returned 2 sporting guns (German) to General Kelly. Three lorries on Colour belts. No truck. One lorries to Fetch 132 rifles from 800th Effrenn.	
"	27.7.19		No trucks	

WAR DIARY
or
INTELLIGENCE SUMMARY.

Army Form C. 2118.

Place	Date	Hour	Summary of Events and Information	Remarks and references to Appendices
Bonn	28.7.19		Visited C.O.O. Coln and got permission to draw tent-bottoms for 52nd Manchesters (70) & Kensington Coln: p (111) on 29.5. Obtained authority from A.O.O. to draw 500 Palliasses.	
"	29.7.19		18 lorries to Coln to draw tent bottoms & 500 hemp pallies. One lorry for palliasses from O.O.F.C.T. delivered to 52 Manchesters. Coln sent only nine III tent bottoms. 70 delivered 52 Manchesters. 30% Kensington. Visited 92 2A, A.O.O., O.O.F.C.T. & drew 120 straps for Lewis guns. Stable necessaries. One truck with KT body for 32 M.G.C. 2 bodies & one bucket KT for 52 Man.	
"	30.7.19		Visited Cop. Coln re balance of tent bottoms. 1 lorry, 50 army artfs [from O.O.T.C.T.] Three lorries on blankets & two lorries drawing stable necessaries for C.O. 8 lorries to Köln to draw 86 tent bottoms (81 delivered to Kensington Coln) 3 " " horse shoes & necessaries. 1 " " Returned bomaries to Siegburg.	

Sgd. [signature]
Davos Kameras

Army Form C. 2118.

WAR DIARY
or
INTELLIGENCE SUMMARY.
(Erase heading not required.)

Instructions regarding War Diaries and Intelligence Summaries are contained in F. S. Regs., Part II. and the Staff Manual respectively. Title pages will be prepared in manuscript.

R.A.O.S.

Place	Date	Hour	Summary of Events and Information	Remarks and references to Appendices
BONN	1.8.19.		One lorry K.T. with body K.T. for 16 L.F. 3 lorries to Coln to collect Boots necessaries. 3 " on Blanket exchange. Visited 3rd T.M.B. went to Refilling point 3rd Bde re exchange of blankets.	
"	2.8.19.		One lorry with marquees (2) to 52nd Manchester. One lorries on blankets. Three lorries visited ore ceded stores to collect stores for exchange, carrying Lt. Morton. Went 69 > 2 T.M.B. see late G.B.n of 90 J.M. re Gt 98 of ambulance units (90 J.M.)	
"	3.8.19		Visited ATSOS Corps. One lorry with 670 blankets to 3rd Bde Refilling point.	
	4.8.19		Visited Field Cashier. A/t. H. Kaithwaite took over Infant account. Major L.H. Pevelee proceeded on leave. Collected 1.9 stats from OO Corps Troops. One lorry to Siegburg for tents but returned empty. One lorry to John ft Jailkasse but Ordnance was shut. Office closed in afternoon	
	5.8.19			

D.D. & L., London, E.C.

WAR DIARY
or
INTELLIGENCE SUMMARY.

(Erase heading not required.)

Army Form C. 2118.

Instructions regarding War Diaries and Intelligence Summaries are contained in F. S. Regs., Part II. and the Staff Manual respectively. Title pages will be prepared in manuscript.

Place	Date	Hour	Summary of Events and Information	Remarks and references to Appendices
BONN	5-8-19		Went to Siegburg. Saw DADOS Eastern Division. Visited ADOS I Corps. One lorry drew Bullasses to Köln. One lorry Harness & Saddlery from I Corps Troops. One lorry on Salvage Bodts Köln. Three lorries on Blankets. One lorry on Salvage from Siegburg.	
	6-8-19		Three lorries on Blankets from Köln. Visited 3rd Bde Salvage 51st Manitoba.	
BONN	7-8-19		Five lorries on Blankets. One on Salvage to Motor Siegburg. Visited ADOS I Corps, I.C.S. M.G. Branch, & Staff Captain 1st Bde.	
	8-8-19		4 lorries went to D Block Köln drawing equipment & necessaries. 3 lorries on Blankets.	
	9-8-19		Three lorries on Blankets. Two lorries to Siegburg with Salvage. Visited 12th L.H. lorries re S.B. Second Bn. I. COO indents to be. B.D. DOS Eastern Division.	
	10-8-19		Sent 362 Blankets to 2nd Bde. Visited ADOS Corps re Eastern Division Stores & Indents to be cancelled re BPR No 346 QD a/4/6/7 - 2 lorries to Köln Blankets - 2 Rugs & Indents to ES.	

WAR DIARY
or
INTELLIGENCE SUMMARY.
(Erase heading not required.)

Army Form C. 2118.

Place	Date	Hour	Summary of Events and Information	Remarks and references to Appendices
Boun.	12.8.19		Lorries. 2 Blankets, 3 Horse Rugs, 4 IGS, 4 Tents to 57SP/KLR. Visited by Bde & Bot KLR.	
"	13.8.19		Lorries - 5 on Eqpt front to Kilh which was returned. 1 Blankets & Tentage to 57Sh Kings City Regt. Visited AD Ordnance II Corps.	
"	14.8.19		Lorries - 2 on Blankets. 2 Stores from Kilh. 2 Salvage to Steghers. Visited DOS Kilh & Regimekins. No Blankets were exchanged.	
"	15.8.19		Lorries - 4 went to Kilh for Stores	
"	16.8.19		One lorry on return 61 CSI Corps. Visited 2nd Bde & Tentage Collec. C.O.O. Kilh & DADOS Eastern Division	
"	17.8.19 18.8.19		lorries - 1 here on stores etc. One Stores trop on Kilh. One Wgn 95 to bring kit to DAQMG Collected Mess eqpt from Steghers. Visited Eastern Division Dumps 16" L Hrs & ADOS II morning. Cpt in afternoon.	
"	19.8.19		Lorries - Three to Kilh for Blankets. None exchanged with units. One to Kilh with gloves & back mit. carts. One with horse & harn from Kilh.	

Army Form C. 2118.

WAR DIARY
or
INTELLIGENCE SUMMARY.
(Erase heading not required.)

Instructions regarding War Diaries and Intelligence Summaries are contained in F. S. Regs. Part II. and the Staff Manual respectively. Title pages will be prepared in manuscript.

Place	Date	Hour	Summary of Events and Information	Remarks and references to Appendices
Bonn	20.8.19		Lorries - One to I.C.B. X on Standards, not Blankets. Visited COO Köln & OC Divisional Train R.A.S.C.	
"	21.8.19		Lorries. Three in town Köln. Three on Blankets to Köln. Visited Dmnt of BRADOS Eastern Division & 3rd Bde.	
"	22.8.19		Lorries. Five went to Köln with 14 equipment & returned with Stores. Visited Major Dunn 11th Lrs in Lohrberg. COO Köln & C. & D front for stones & lumber, which was allowed to OC 2nd Train.	
"	23.8.19		Visited M.E.Bn., D.A.P.M. Siegburg Tuesday & Eastern Div Dumps. 2 Lorries went to Siegburg with stores.	
"	24.8.19		Visited A.D.O.S. X Corps. One lorries to town & to 'Q' Branch.	
"	25.8.19		Visited C/161 By R.F.A. Siegburg Dmnt. & 51st Kings Liverpool. Lorries - Bonn Standards - 1 to Siegburg. 2 on 9 order 1 Rahm. Visited Siegburg Dmnt., C.OO Cologne + O.O. Cologne. Lorries - 4 to Siegburg Dmnt. + 1 Rahm	
"	27.8.19		Three lorries with Kings horse from SOS & F 90 station	

WAR DIARY
or
INTELLIGENCE SUMMARY.

Army Form C. 2118.

Place	Date	Hour	Summary of Events and Information	Remarks and references to Appendices
BONN	28.8.19		Five lorries 4.30 a.m. w/shops to clear carriages (8 pdr) a return to Euskirchen. Railhead moved to Bonn H. Arrangements made to K-B to and stores by rail in future. 2 lorries on blankets held as K-B to and stores by rail in future.	
"	29.8.19		30v salvage. 1 on 3 GSW 6 IAS (no cat available). Three lorries on horse rugs to Köln. One lorry to collect garments etc from Vilsham (no car available)	
"	30.8.19		Visited ASD & Corps. Eastern Div dump Siegburg. One lorry with "D" M.T. Body.	
"	31.8.19		Remained in office.	

Sd Archer Maj
Danos Lancs Div

WAR DIARY
or
INTELLIGENCE SUMMARY.
(Erase heading not required.)

Army Form C. 2118.

D.A.D.O.S., LANCASHIRE DIVISION

Place	Date	Hour	Summary of Events and Information	Remarks and references to Appendices
BONN	1.9.19		Visited Coo Köln and returned flags borrowed by Div for Horseshow.	
"	2.9.19		Visited Siegberg (DADOS Eastern Div Group) and 4 Coy of Train, 3rd Bde. Helofs and I.C.S. X Corps. No truck. Two lorries on draw up to Köln & on returned Ordnance.	
"	3.9.19		No truck. Three loads wheels & horseshoe to Rathenow.	
"	4.9.19		One truck 5 tons received. Visited Siegberg to bring back Mr Fairthwaite. Visited 57th Manchesters.	
"	5.9.19		Was wakened at 02.00 hrs and informed the dump was on fire. When I got to the dump (02.05 hrs) I found the dump of Enclave Box Rations Equipment was on fire. The German fire engine was in action and Major Dunham & BETMc was in charge. The alarm had been given by some officer (at present unknown) about 01.30 hrs. The fire engine arrived about 01.30 hrs. The fire was finally extinguished about 04.30 hrs. Fleut. Fairthwaite and a guard of 6 men were left to watch till daylight. No trucks. Three lorries blankets & three lorries moving equipment from Stores to X Inf. I.C.S. ADOS X Corps & AA + QMG Division visited scene of fire. Visited I.C.S. & damage of 16 equipment.	

Army Form C. 2118.

WAR DIARY
or
INTELLIGENCE SUMMARY.
(Erase heading not required.)

Instructions regarding War Diaries and Intelligence Summaries are contained in F.S. Regs., Part II. and the Staff Manual respectively. Title pages will be prepared in manuscript.

Place	Date	Hour	Summary of Events and Information	Remarks and references to Appendices
BOHN	6.9.19		Visited 15th Armn. Another 6/9505 X Co/s. No trucks in Six lorries moving serviceable equipment to Impels.	
"	7.9.19		Nil.	
"	8.9.19		Visited D.A.C. & C.O.O. Köln — No trucks in yard only lorries — Three removing 7 wheeler to I.C.S. & two removing stores to run stores in Pippelsdorf Alle.	
"	9.9.19		Visited 204th, 219 Field Coys. R.E. & 92nd & 7 Ambulances 210S that lorries mend stores to ICS. No trucks in yard.	
"	10.9.19		No truck. No car available. Lorries employed shifting dumps to 75 Pippelsdorfer Allee. Two trucks of Celo, Grey, Oak, Oil, grass, macaroni. Spread ICS 218 Field Coy, 9 F.A. & 2nd BdeT.M.B.	
"	11.9.19		Visited ICS 218 Field Coy. 9 F.A. & 2nd Bde T.M.B.	
"	12.9.19		Visited 164 F.F. Collected duty Markels (1900) from MGB.	
"	13.9.19		Unit drawing. Visited A.O.D. No car available. One lorry.	
"	14.9.19		200 trucks. Two lorries.	
"	15.9.19		Visited Hd Qrs A,B,C,D 168 Bde R.F.A. 1st Bn Halifs & 5 Kings. 2nd Bde Hd Qrs. two lorries & stores to ICS from RTO Siegburg. Three lorries on Han Huts.	

Army Form C. 2118.

WAR DIARY
or
INTELLIGENCE SUMMARY.
(Erase heading not required.)

Instructions regarding War Diaries and Intelligence Summaries are contained in F.S. Regs., Part II. and the Staff Manual respectively. Title pages will be prepared in manuscript.

Place	Date	Hour	Summary of Events and Information	Remarks and references to Appendices
BONN	16.9.19		No lunch. No car. Visited I.C.S. with ADOS II Corps. Visited Kennebergcamp with Dagong Batmy. moved beds from VII Cn. to L.H.Dmn. One lorry returned to 12" LH tram R. forward station	
	17.9.19		Visited 51st King's L Rgt + 12" L.H. tram R.t (mmf) Inquiry held on fire which occurred on the 5th inst — one shell pulverised to 12" L.H.tm. two armoured railway to I.C.O.	
	18.9.19		Visited HQ Port Bola Three lorries moved Stores from Railhead to Damp.	
	19.9.19		Visited M.G. Con. 5th Manchester. Two lorries returned clothes to "B" group. One to I.C.S. No trucks.	
	20.9.19		Visited Mendorf to pick up M.g.tm. Stores. Could not find them.	
	21.9.19		Nil	
	22.9.19		Visited I.C.S. ADOS II Corps 51st Manitoba + 5th Manitoba. Three lorries removed salvage to Shops I.C.S. No trucks	
	23.9.19		Visited I.C.S.	

WAR DIARY
or
INTELLIGENCE SUMMARY.
(Erase heading not required.)

Army Form C. 2118.

Place	Date	Hour	Summary of Events and Information	Remarks and references to Appendices
Basra	24.9.19		Visited 32nd M.G.Bn. 52nd Br. Manchesters 15th & 16th hand. Fire fighting Fatigue party at I.C.S. sorting equipment. Two lorries to I.C.S. No trucks	
	25.9.19		Visited H.Q. A.B.C + D. Batteries 161st Bde R.F.A. No 4 Coy Bn. train 32nd M.G.Bn. + 51st & 52nd Manchester + I.C.S. IV C.T. + A.Sors X Inf. One lorry to I.C.S. No trucks	
	26.9.19		Visited HEMMERICH & abandoned Stokes Mortar, 6000 Kilos, 00 7mm.m.kms. E/ S/ gun f. Holmes fire extinguishers & ladders. Sent five lorries to 00 7 am it with 08 & 14 Smythe equipment. Drew two extinguishers & thump drain (?). Three lorries to IV Three lorries empty and moving stores. Three trucks. Three lorries moved returns to dump. Visited I.C.S.	
	28.9.19		Nil	
	29.9.19		Visited I.C.S, 5th Borders 2nd Bde Arty B/o 139 & 57th Kings 1st T.M.B. 2 Coy from Mobile City section and 12 L N vans. No trucks. One lorry to I.C.S	
	30.9.19		Visited .... Two lorries to I.C.S	

Jno Purchas Capt
Capn Lancs RE

WAR DIARY
or
INTELLIGENCE SUMMARY.
(Erase heading not required.)

Army Form C. 2118.

October, 1919.

Place	Date	Hour	Summary of Events and Information	Remarks and references to Appendices
BONN GERMANY	1.10.19		Visited Technical College SIEGBURG. No trucks. Two lorries 6 I.C.S.	
	2.X.19		Visited I.C.S. Two lorries to I.C.S. No trucks	
	3.X.19		One lorry to I.C.S. No trucks. Major Paxton proceeded on leave. One truck. Two lorries removed stores from reichbahn?	
	4.X.19		Visited A.D.O.S II Corps re requisitioning of leather. No truck.	
	5.X.19		Visited Requisition Officer Bonn re different Wg in getting tool & limbers. Part of Pl...	
	6.X.19		Visited Commdt. Mot. ÜBERCASSEL & collected detonators & Technical College SIEGBURG to obtain regulations. No truck. One lorry to I.C.S	
	7.X.19		Visited by A.D.O.S II Corps. Visited Military Prison SIEGBURG. No & Coy Disl. Train. No truck. One lorry sent to With with blankets for Manning	
	8.X.19		Visited HQ Coy train. I.C.S. II Corps. One lorry to I.D.S. No truck	
	9.X.19		Visited I.C.S. A.D.O.S. Coct & D'qmmt M.T.R. One lorry to I.C.S. No truck	
	10.X.19		Visited I.C.S II Corps Ammunition Depot Q.Z. Hela Tallyzl within Honorav 12NEunn, Sit Rwhlny... ??? 21 prist ... I.C.S One truck. Two lorries am stores Ergersellthale. Visited I.C.S Ergersellthale.	
	11.X.19			
	12.X.19		Two truck, three lorry loads equipment 15 TMh from I.C.S Ergerssellthale Drew Equipment	
	13.X.19		No truck. No car.	
	14.X.19		Visited Army Advisor at I.C.S. No truck.	
	15.X.19		One truck R detail stores only.	
	16.X.19		No truck	
	17.X.19			

WAR DIARY
or
INTELLIGENCE SUMMARY.
(Erase heading not required.)

Army Form C. 2118.

Instructions regarding War Diaries and Intelligence Summaries are contained in F.S. Regs. Part II. and the Staff Manual respectively. Title pages will be prepared in manuscript.

Place	Date	Hour	Summary of Events and Information	Remarks and references to Appendices
Bonn	18.10.19		No turnout	
"	19.10.19		No turnout.	
"	20.10.19		Bunch of horseshoes. Visited A.D.O.S. VI Corps & Home 58 Shelander hfr re horses.	
"	21.10.19		Visited Home No. 6 9 R.O.S. 2nd Bn H.Q.	
"	22.10.19		Incorporated handing in camp Returns 2 – 4 – 9 – 12. Spent the day at I.C.S.	
"	23.10.19		Unit continued handing in. Visited Cookham a E.g.t. re issue of Winter underclothing to 52 Kings, but struck off nothing arrived.	
"	24.10.19		Visited I.C.S. Cookham + hipper re Lewis gun shots for 52 Kings. Clerks not available.	
"	25.10.19		200 to nice to Home to collect cases W.P.	
"	26.10.19		Money opened Office from 10.00 – 12.00 hrs (Sunday)	
"	27.10.19		Visited I.C.S., A.O.O. Cookham re bicycle parts for 5 Kings.	
"	28.10.19		Visited I.C.S. one lorry total to collect stores for 52 Whips.	
"	29.10.19		Visited I.C.S. Job of 92. Body H.L. transferred all units to 67 C.T.	
"	30.10.19		One lorry to 12 & Co., Paym'r H.Q. ordnance Sent to 00 E.C.T. Visited A.O.S. 67 Manchester N.C.S.	
"	31.10.19		Visited M.G.C. & Returned stores to 7 C.S.I.	

Two Finches M.A. 2nd Bn Kings Rgt.

R.W.D.

WAR DIARY
or
INTELLIGENCE SUMMARY.
(Erase heading not required.)

Army Form C. 2118.

Instructions regarding War Diaries and Intelligence Summaries are contained in F. S. Regs., Part II. and the Staff Manual respectively. Title pages will be prepared in manuscript.

Place	Date	Hour	Summary of Events and Information	Remarks and references to Appendices
BONN	1.11.19		Visited I.C.S. Staff Offices & T.C.S. Units moved O.O. & C.G.	
	2.11.19		Sunday.	
	3.11.19		Visited Siegberg railhead dump. Cookers C/O group & T.C.S.	
	4.11.19		Visited " " " with paint for utensils. & O.O.T.C.S.	
	5.11.19		No car available. Old dump being cleared up.	
	6.11.19		Vis. led I.C.S. " "	
	7.11.19		Vis. led Town Major's office BEUEL.	
	8.11.19		No car.	
	9.11.19		Sunday.	
	10.11.19		Visited J.C.O.O. kidents O.O. Clothing 20 Hot Sgn. Hospl & C.R.E. I.C.S. I. cafes.	
	11.11.19		Remained in office. 2 mins silence at 11.00 hrs	
	12.11.19		Visited I.C.S.O.S Ring	
	13.11.19		Lorry load of stores collected from Beuel & delivered to T.C.S. Great stores held been abandoned by troops.	
	14.11.19		Sent both lorries to T.C.S	
	15.11.19		Visited I.C.S. 9.52 Manchesters & A.S.O.	
	16.11.19		Sunday	

WAR DIARY
or
INTELLIGENCE SUMMARY

Army Form C. 2118.

Place	Date	Hour	Summary of Events and Information	Remarks and references to Appendices
BONN	17.11.19		Visited Railhead (a name of rations) I.C.S. A.P.O.	
"	18.11.19		Visited Lt Sammo Siegberg re drying of tents of 52nd Manchesters. Rott & found some Bananda Stores all RE equipmnt. 35 pieces of Antbottoms. Rifle range DAM B Roien's found Latrine buckets. Visited I.C.S.	+ See any 496 24/8.11.19
	19.11.19		Visited mess Lt Sammo Siegberg a 52nd Manchesters.	
	20.11.19		Visited I.C.S. Sent lorry to I.C.S.	
	21.11.19		Visited Railhead dump at Siegberg re numbers of Ammo Carriages. Visited O-s-D g/P Rott re Flags lost out. At threshold Bunn lorry 52nd Manchesters to take tents to Siegberg for drying. Lorry broke down & arrived too late.	
	22.11.19		Visited Siegberg Railhead dump at Empire Store, Army 52nd Manchesters to take tents to Siegberg. Lorry sent to I.C.S. Answered for A.P.O. & O/c.	
	23.11.19		Sunday	
	24.11.19		Visited Bonn & Siegberg dumps to obtain required nos of guns etc. Visited MENDEN. no stores appear to have been left. Visited I.C.S.	

Army Form C. 2118.

WAR DIARY
or
INTELLIGENCE SUMMARY.
(Erase heading not required.)

Instructions regarding War Diaries and Intelligence Summaries are contained in F. S. Regs., Part II. and the Staff Manual respectively. Title pages will be prepared in manuscript.

Place	Date	Hour	Summary of Events and Information	Remarks and references to Appendices
BONN	25.11.19		Visited 5 Kings ADMS. Visited Town Major Godesberg. Visited Meckear and found 5 Stores dept and 2 Motor Amb & German travelling Kitchens abandoned by 195 Siege Battery	
"	26.11.19		Visited BEUEL & GODESBERG. No appearance of ornalike store. Visited ICP. 2 Lorries to TCS.	
"	27.11.19		Visited ICP, ADMS & Endenich (no reintroduction of Gunnar). Railhead. 1 Lorry to TCS.	
"	28.11.19		Stayed in Office	
"	29.11.19		Visited TCS. & 2 Kings & ADMS	
"	30.11.19		Sunday	

JMSAuchan Lt/Col
ADMS Lancaster)

www.ingramcontent.com/pod-product-compliance
Lightning Source LLC
Chambersburg PA
CBHW081458160426
43193CB00013B/2524